Stress and Freedom

D1235053

Stress and Freedom

Peter Sloterdijk

Translated by Wieland Hoban

polity

First published in German as *Streß und Freiheit*, © Suhrkamp Verlag, Berlin, 2011

This English edition © Polity Press, 2016

Polity Press
65 Bridge Street
Cambridge CB2 1UR, UK

Polity Press
350 Main Street
Malden, MA 02148, USA

All rights reserved. Except for the quotation of short passages for the purpose of criticism and review, no part of this publication may be reproduced, stored in a retrieval system, or transmitted, in any form or by any means, electronic, mechanical, photocopying, recording or otherwise, without the prior permission of the publisher.

ISBN-13: 978-0-7456-9928-8 (hardback)
ISBN-13: 978-0-7456-9929-5 (paperback)

A catalogue record for this book is available from the British Library.

Library of Congress Cataloging-in-Publication Data

Sloterdijk, Peter, 1947–
[Stress und Freiheit. English]
Stress and freedom / Peter Sloterdijk.
pages cm
ISBN 978-0-7456-9928-8 (hardback) -- ISBN 978-0-7456-9929-5 (pbk.) 1. Stress (Psychology). 2. Liberty--Philosophy. 3. Stress (Psychology)--Social aspects. 4. Liberty--Social aspects. I. Title.
BF575.S75S57513 2015
123'.5--dc23
2015019454

Typeset in 12.5 on 15 pt Adobe Garamond by
Servis Filmsetting Ltd, Stockport, Cheshire
Printed and bound in Great Britain by Clays Limited, St Ives PLC

The publisher has used its best endeavours to ensure that the URLs for external websites referred to in this book are correct and active at the time of going to press. However, the publisher has no responsibility for the websites and can make no guarantee that a site will remain live or that the content is or will remain appropriate.

Every effort has been made to trace all copyright holders, but if any have been inadvertently overlooked the publisher will be pleased to include any necessary credits in any subsequent reprint or edition.

For further information on Polity, visit our website: politybooks.com

Contents

Note

The present text reproduces a speech given on 6 April 2011 at the invitation of the Friedrich Naumann Foundation for Freedom as part of the Berlin Speeches on Freedom. The author extends very warm thanks to Katrin Burkhardt, Director of the Berlin branch of the Allianz SE, and Wolfgang Gerhardt, President of the Friedrich Naumann Foundation for Freedom, for their hospitality.

philosophical and academic literature for almost fifty years and becoming acquainted with a substantial number of authors in various fields of knowledge – be it as a reader or through personal encounters – I have never met anyone, perhaps with one exception, of whom one could seriously claim that the origin of their intellectual activities had been a sense of wonder. On the contrary, it seems as though organized scholarship and instutionalized philosophy has assumed the form of a campaign against amazement. The knowing personnel, the actors in the campaign, have long hidden behind the mask of unimpressability – this has occasionally been termed 'resistance to astonishment'. On the whole, the current culture of knowledge has entirely appropriated the stance of the Stoics' *nihil admirari*: though ancient wisdom teaching impressed upon its adepts the rule of no longer being amazed by anything, the maxim only reached its goal in modern times. In the seventeenth century, Descartes characterized *estonnement* as a thoroughly negative affectation of the mind, a highly unpleasant and unwelcome confusion to be overcome through intellectual effort.[3] The development of our cultures of rationality agreed with its co-founder on this

2

point. If there is still any trace in our time of that supposedly original *thaumazein*, the astonished pause for reflection before an unheard-of object, one can be sure that it is attributable to an outside voice or the words of a layperson; the experts shrug and return to business as usual.

Nowhere is this more apparent than in the social sciences. According to their own internal standards they can be described as a resolutely wonder-free zone. If one gives it some thought, this is a bizarre finding; for if there is anything that could unconditionally demand the amazement of laypersons and the astonishment of scholars, it is the existence of those large political bodies that were formerly known as 'peoples' and are now, thanks to a questionable semantic convention, termed 'societies'. Usually the word calls to mind large or very large political entities with a demographic volume of between several million and over a billion members. Nothing should be more amazing than the ability of these ensembles

---

[3] René Descartes, *The Passions of the Soul*, trans. Stephen H. Voss (Indianapolis: Hackett, 1989), Article 73 (p. 58): 'Astonishment is an excess of wonder which can never be anything but bad.'

of millions and billions of humans to exist in their national-cultural shells with their manifold internal divisions. We should be astonished by these standing armies of political groups which – one does not know how – succeed time and again in convincing their members that their shared situation and history tied their destinies to one another as shareholders, and thus legal comrades and participants in local survival projects. The astonishing nature of these objects crosses the boundary to the inconceivable as soon as we consider that more than a few of the large-scale political bodies in recent history – since the beginnings of the liberal Western cultures in the seventeenth century, shall we say – are formed by populations with growing individualistic tendencies. What I mean here by individualism is the life form that loosens the embeddedness of individuals in collectives, and questions the seemingly immemorial absolutism of the shared by assigning to every single human the dignity of being absolutely *sui generis*. Nothing is more amazing than the survival of civilizations whose members predominantly hold the conviction that their own existence is one dimension realer than everything surrounding them on the side of the collective.

4

In the following, I would like to carry out – against the main current of non-wondering political science and sociology – an exercise in amazement that will be concerned with doing slightly more justice to the unfathomably astonishing nature of contemporary life forms. A civilization such as ours, which rests on the integration of individualistic populations in gigantic large-scale political bodies, is an actually existing maximum improbability. We consign the existence of unicorns to the realm of fables, but accept the notion of an actually existing million-headed fantasy creature 'society' as if it were a self-evident reality. It is, however, understood that the stability of these great constructs is not guaranteed. The shareholders themselves increasingly view the tenability of their current life forms as problematic. Were this not the case, the elites in the social subsystems would not have been for some time incessantly discussing the sustainability of their *modus vivendi*. The word 'sustainability' is undoubtedly the central semantic symptom of the current cultural crisis: it crops up everywhere in the speeches of responsible parties like a neurotic tic pointing to unresolved tensions in their drive systems. It is a reaction to an unease that

5

lective that succeeds in jointly keeping uncalm. Within it, a constant, varyingly intense flow of stress topics must ensure the synchronization of consciousnesses in order to integrate the respective population into a community of concern and excitation that regenerates from day to day. That is why modern information media are simply indispensable for the creation of coherence in national and continental stress communes. They alone are capable of binding together the diverging collectives with counter-tensions using a constant flow of irritant topics. The function of the media in stress-integrated multi-milieu society lies in evoking and provoking the collectives as such by making new excitation suggestions to them on a daily and hourly basis – suggestions of outrage, envy or presumption, a wealth of offers directed at the sentimentality, willingness for fear and indiscretion of the shareholders. Every day, the recipients choose from these. The nation is a daily plebiscite – but about the priority of concerns, not about the constitution. By selecting the best possibilities for synchronous excitations, the large-scale groups vibrating in constant nervousness reproduce the ether of commonality without which social cohesion – or even the mere

2

Lucretia's Revolt, Rousseau's Retreat

It is in the nature of the matter that when thinking about social synthesis through group stress,
one will come up against the problem of freedom
sooner or later. In the following, the concept of
freedom will be addressed first of all in its ancient
meaning, which should by no means be confused
with modern interpretations of the word. I will
begin by calling to mind a primal scene from
the Old European political tradition that dem-
onstrates the original connection between stress
and freedom with archetypal clarity. After that,
I will introduce a contrasting modern scene that
presents the same connection in an entirely different light.

In the first book of *Ab urbe condita*, Livy

recounts how it came to pass that the Romans one day shook off the yoke of Etruscan–Tarquinian rule and founded the *res publica*, which, together with certain borrowings from Classical Greek urban culture, supplies the historical model for solidary civil societies to this day.[4] The scene took place around 509 BC. A small Roman–Etruscan army is besieging the city of Ardea, some thirty-five kilometres south of Rome. One evening, officers gather in a tent and do what men afield cannot help doing: they speak about women, specifically their own wives, with eager sideways glances at one another. Collatinus stands out for his endless effusion about the beauty and virtue of his wife Lucretia. The other officers are more inclined to take the primal Etruscan view that *La donna è mobile*. The group decides to leave for Rome in order to observe the behaviour of the matrons in the absence of their husbands. And indeed: they find their wives engaged in rather un-ladylike amusements, while Lucretia alone is sitting among her handmaidens spinning flax. She wins the prize of virtue, but also that of desir-

[4] Livy, *The History of Rome, Books 1-5*, trans. Valerie M. Warrior (Indianapolis: Hackett, 2006), Book I, 58-60 (pp. 80-3).

and the tyrants are driven out; never again will a single arrogant man be at the head of the Roman body politic. Let me highlight the point of this story in the context of these reflections: the account deals with no less than the birth of republican freedom from collective outrage. That sentiment transforms all those involved into an aggressive stress group, which in turn becomes a political commune. The first great political affect with liberal and republican tendencies found its central issue in the rejection of a shameful act. When political freedom reached European soil, it did so in an outburst of rage shared by thousands. (The arrogance of power often manifests itself not only in the tyrants themselves, but also among the sons born into the same presumption – in antiquity as today, whether the noxious paternal role models were Tarquin the Proud or Muammar Gaddafi.) The anti-monarchic affect that was a stable feature in the political psychology of the Romans from this primal scene on is not surprising; the mere mention of the word 'king' triggers the most intense aversions among the members of the stalwart patrician republic. Consequently, even the later Caesars had to avoid the title *rex* and conceal their autocracy behind constant references to the authority of the senate and the Roman people. A glance towards Greece shows how there too, it was an anti-tyrannical front that first established an awareness of freedom. What the Greeks called *eleuthería* – a word that is conventionally translated as 'freedom', evoking numerous misunderstandings – initially meant no more than the longing to live in an autochthonous (self-growing) fashion (following the *patrioi nomoi*, the laws of the fathers) among their own people and not being subject to the despotic (house-masterly) wilfulness of an individual who had become outsized – especially to the rule of the Persian Great Kings. In this sense, the battles of Marathon, Salamis and Plataea were freedom wars.

From a freedom-historical perspective, the Lucretia revolt and the victories of the Greeks are connected. Neither case should be associated with 'freedom movements' in the modern sense. The Romans and the Greeks were equally uninterested in human rights and freedom of opinion – although the Greek praise of verbal candour between men, *parrhesía*, which literally means 'saying everything', was an early foreshadowing of what would later be enshrined in law as freedom of expression. But the Greek verbal courage is far more an aspect of the agonal cult and an extension of the athletic will to compete that has been transferred to the sphere of speech about truth than a political right or civil virtue. The subject of ancient freedom is the people – more precisely, the complex of *demos* and *ethos* that forms a *polis*. To give the matter the appropriate emphasis, one should say that freedom here is nothing other than the right of a collective to ethnic self-enclosure. It refers to the prerogative of being guided by nothing but habits, customs and institutions that have shaped the members of the collective since youth. Thus freedom here means the spontaneous consent of an ethnic group to the beloved despotism of their traditions. This formulation indicates the inner boundary of the ancient or ethnic understanding of freedom. For if freedom only means the option for the undisturbed possession of a collective by their own conventions, it is clear why such a view cannot persist once individuals appear who question the commanding power of custom, indeed the 'morality of custom' itself.[5]

[5] Cf. Friedrich Nietzsche, *Daybreak*, trans. R. J. Hollingdale (Cambridge University Press, 1997), p. 10.

Peoples may view themselves as sovereign in the legal sense, and indeed they mostly do in post-imperial times. In the civilization-theoretical sense, however, they are incapable of sovereignty because the ethnic element as such results in a narrow-minded insistence on the conventional. When a reflective individual appears on the scene, breaking away from the dominion of collective customs and making itself subject to a higher law – be it Nature, a faith illuminated by a holy text, or the individual law of the search for happiness – research into the meaning of freedom is set in motion.

The second primal scene in the unfolding of the European concept of freedom of which I intend to speak here took place on Swiss soil over two thousand years later, in the autumn of 1765. Thanks to its sole witness, who was at once the main figure in the events, our knowledge about it is relatively extensive. By that time, Switzerland had long played a part in the history of the renewed republican idea of freedom, but – as I will show presently – taken on an equally significant role in the history of modern subjectivity, which was picking up speed at the time. The hero of the story is none other than the Geneva-born

Jean-Jacques Rousseau, aged fifty-three in that year, a man on the run. A European celebrity since the age of forty, when he had been awarded the prize of the Lyon Academy, he rose to the status of a scandalous figure after such literary successes as *Julie, or the New Heloise* (1761, with almost a hundred printings by 1800), *The Social Contract* (1762) and *Émile* (1762). In today's terminology one would say that he achieved promotion from being a star to a superstar. In particular, the most fascinating piece from *Émile*, 'The Creed of a Savoyard Priest', which was read as the manifesto of a pantheistic religion of the heart, won its author the enmity of the Parisian high clergy and the Geneva establishment. Warrants for his arrest were issued and permits of residence were revoked. During the night of 6 September 1765, an anonymous rabble threw stones at Rousseau's residence in Môtiers, in the then-Prussian canton of Neuchâtel – a event the author still described twelve years later as a 'stoning' (*lapidation*).[6] Amazingly enough, it never occurred to him

[6] Jean-Jacques Rousseau, *Reveries of the Solitary Walker*, trans. Russell Goulborne (Oxford and New York: Oxford University Press, 2011), p. 50. Cf. also *The Confessions*, Book 12.

that he might have provoked these attacks through his own behaviour. In Môtiers he had presented himself in the costume of a travelling Armenian, wearing a dressing gown-like caftan and a cheeky fur cap. This recalls other media stars of the last century and the present day, for whom any outfit is acceptable to emphasize that they are different. In summary, one can probably say that Rousseau never understood the laws of modern celebrity. Nonetheless, he has a place of honour in the history of incipient mass culture. He was not the first world-famous person to end their career in bitterness. He deserves an even greater place of honour in the history of psychology: he was the chief witness for the realization that there are paranoiacs who are genuinely persecuted.

In his difficult situation, Rousseau decided to withdraw to an almost deserted island in the middle of Lake Biel, together with his indispensable, tyrannically admiring companion Marie-Thérèse Le Vasseur. Diligent biographers have established precisely the dates of his sojourn on St Peter's Island, which lasted from 12 September to 25 October 1765 – the island soon became a place of pilgrimage for Rousseau admirers. Those days are of great significance for the history of ideas, because something resembling the Big Bang took place for the modern poetry of subjectivity, which turned directly into the philosophy of freedom – if one can believe the author's account in *Reveries of the Solitary Walker* of 1776/77. I must immediately withdraw the phrase 'Big Bang', however, as it was not in fact an explosive event, but rather an almost imperceptible one of a more *im*plosive or contemplative character. Rousseau gave a vivid description of the scene in his legendary 'Fifth Walk' from the *Reveries*. On some sunny autumn days the persecuted author, by now settled down and enchanted by the charm of the quiet island, rowed out onto the lake. Somewhere far out, he put down the oars and lay down in the boat on his back to indulge in his favourite activity: he surrendered to an inner drifting for which the author used the word *rêverie*. One could also describe this flowing of the soul without clinging to any one topic as an immaterial meditation – in the European rather than the Far Eastern sense. Rousseau himself says that at times he let himself drift for hours, immersed in reveries that had no real object, yet were a thousand times sweeter for him than all the things usually known as the pleasures of life.[7] He often approached the point where he was ready to say, 'I wish this moment would last forever.' In his intentionless drifting he discovered the pure psychological duration, in which the conventional course of time with its memories and anticipations disappears, making room for a flowing succession of now-moments uncorrupted by any flaws and undisturbed by any thoughts of absent things.

It is worth letting the author speak so that we can hear how he comments on his self-discovery on the threshold between self-loss and self-appropriation. Here he succeeds in making bold generalizations that would become significant for the history of modern subjectivity, and *eo ipso* for modern freedom tendencies.

What does one enjoy in such a situation? Nothing external to the self, nothing but oneself and one's own existence: as long as this state lasts, one is self-sufficient like God. The feeling of existence stripped of all other affections is in itself a precious feeling of contentment and peace which alone

[7] Rousseau, *Reveries of the Solitary Walker*, p. 53.

would be enough to make this existence prized and cherished by anyone who could banish all the sensual and earthly impressions which constantly distract us from it and upset the joy of it in this world.[8]

The reader of today will probably have some difficulty relating to the still sensation that manifests itself in these lines. It was not lost on Rousseau's contemporaries. The words convey no less than the first appearance of a concept of existence in which the modern individual enters the scene. This individual at once presents itself as a new subject of freedom. This primal scene of existential thought reveals that the new freedom of 1765 was not yet a freedom for entrepreneurs, explorers or authors. The author specifically emphasizes that *in situ* he was initially uninterested in a licence for a literary expression of his inner feelings. (Rousseau would later insist that he did not have anything to write with on St Peter's Island, meaning that if something ever needed to be noted down, he had to borrow the island tenant's

[8] Ibid., pp. 55f.

consciousness. In this moment, the concept of freedom involuntarily takes on a new meaning, a meaning that contradicts everything ever associated with it in the past (freedom as the right to be unmolested by arbitrary rule, as a legal cooperative in the *polis*, as individual autarchy, as cult freedom, as the privilege of masters, as the freedom of the Christian and so on). It refers to a state of exquisite unusability in which the individual is entirely with themselves, but mostly detached from their everyday identity. In the freedom of reverie, the individual is far removed from 'society', but also detached from their own person as woven into the social fabric. They leave both things behind: the world of collective themes of concern and themselves as part of it. Hence an individual becomes free through the conquest of carefreeness. Freedom is experienced in the most current sense by those who discover a sublime unemployment within themselves – without having to report to an employment agency. Henceforth, the only people who could call themselves free would be those who succeeded in attending to themselves in such a way that the source of a feeling of existence began to flow inside them – not in the mode of boredom as in Heidegger, nor in the mode of nausea as expounded by Sartre, but with the timbre of a quiet euphoria that manifests an immaterial affirmation of the total situation before any articulated agreement with one or the other. The decisive aspect of these discoveries is the absence of any reference to achievements. The subject of the 'Fifth Walk' is neither a cognitive subject nor a willed, entrepreneurial or political subject. It is not even an artistic subject. It has nothing to say, it has no opinion, it does not express itself and it has no project. It is neither creative nor progressive, nor is it benevolent. Its new freedom is revealed in its ecstatic unusability for any purpose. Rousseau's free human discovers that they are the most useless person in the world – and has no objections whatsoever.

3

Stress and Freedom

These recollections of the two primal scenes in the European history of freedom elucidate how members of Western cultures experience the fact that they must always, either actually or potentially, confront two manifestations of unfreedom. We experience the first form as political oppression and the second as repression by the reality known, rightly or wrongly, as the external. (A third front of unfreedom, resulting from the enslavement of humans by false self-images, does not require discussion in the present context.)

The two primary oppressions can be described as variants of stress experience. Political repression constitutes a stress system that proves successful as long as the oppressed tend more towards avoidance of stress – colloquially put: obedience, submission, willingness to service – than rebellion and revolution. In technical language, an anti-tyrannical revolt means a 'maximal stress cooperation'[9] by the dominated to eliminate an intolerable burden imposed by the dominant. Revolutions break out when collectives intuitively recalculate their stress balance at critical moments and reach the conclusion that existence in the attitude of submissive stress avoidance is ultimately more costly than the stress of rebellion. In the most extreme case, the calculus is this: better dead than enslaved any longer. Where such reckoning catches on, there will be no more tolerance of domination or faith in authority, whether in the short or the long term. One can explain why milder tyrannies last longer from a stress-theoretical perspective: they deprive their subjects of a motive to make such calculations

[9] The concept of Maximal Stress Cooperation (MSC) was first developed in Heiner Mühlmann, *The Nature of Cultures: A Blueprint for a Theory of Culture Genetics*, trans. R. Payne (Vienna and New York: Springer, 1996). In the following, I will consistently refer to the technical concept of stress developed there, but will occasionally also take the liberty of using the term less technically.

by offering sufficiently pleasant compensation for existing under the yoke of subordination. That is why Kant could refer to a paternal government as the 'greatest conceivable despotism",[10] and he was right to the extent that a system of well-meaning patronization is never geared towards emancipation. Liberation from paternalism has its specific price, however. When revolutionaries succeed, they often find that each revolution is followed by the call for a second – not so much because the supporters of the old conditions carry out a counter-revolution, but because those who were not satisfied with the first revolution recalculate their stress balance and conclude that even in the improved social order, the price is still too high. Indeed, they feel the stress all the more keenly because they now measure their burden by raised standards. It almost seems as if all relief effects in modern communities are doomed to be eaten up by heightened sensitizations. The law of increasing discon-

[10] Immanuel Kant, 'On the Common Saying: "This May Be True in Theory, but It Does Not Apply in Practice"', in *Political Writings*, ed. Hans Reiss, trans. H. B. Nisbet (Cambridge University Press, 1991), p. 74.

tent in democracies is still awaiting a systemic explanation.

On the other unfreedom front, people are confronted with the burdening character of reality as such. No one needs to be shown laboriously how it pushes existence down. Nonetheless, Lotario di Segni, the later Pope Innocent III, presented a veritable compendium of burdened life in his treatise *On the Misery of the Human Condition* (*De humanae conditionis miseria*, 1195). One classic of early modern realism was more concise. Thomas Hobbes summarized the course of most people's lives in five fatal attributes: 'solitary, poore, nasty, brutish and short'.[11] When the Old Testament psalmist tells us that even a long, pleasurable life is but 'trouble and sorrow', he is supported by the law of existential gravity known to all mortals. If the saying goes that 'life is hard', this is a laconic but clear reference to the faceless despotism of the real. And when Heidegger speaks of the concern structure of Dasein, he transposes the old folk ontology into a contemporary and academic register. And yet: neither the psalmist nor the saying

[11] Thomas Hobbes, *Leviathan*, ed. Richard Tuck (Cambridge University Press, 1996), p. 89.

nor Heidegger was willing or able to take into account that a revolt against the tyranny of the real has got under way in our part of the world, a revolt that we present under a number of varyingly worn-down names: Industrial Revolution, Enlightenment, modernization, welfare, technology or democracy. Someone using these words does not usually consider that all of them make sense only as parts of an ontological revolution. They name aspects of the epochal revolt against the oppressive burden character of the former reality. Whoever wants to be modern works on turning an existing reality into a former reality – a hard one into a easy one, an implacable one into a negotiable one. The ontological freedom movement we call modernity rests on the fundamental need 'to escape completely from the yoke of circumstances'.[12] This need may well have existed latently since time immemorial, but it was only the modern world that gave it an effective means of satisfaction through technology and welfare culture. Hence the unprecedented nature of the

---

[12] Arnold Gehlen, 'Über die Geburt der Freiheit aus der Entfremdung' (1952), in *Gesamtausgabe*, vol. 4 (Frankfurt: Klostermann, 1983), pp. 366-79, here p. 379.

the same man who, barely three years earlier, had committed to paper the most provocative and seemingly most understandable, yet in reality most muddled statement in political anthropology: 'Man is born free, and everywhere he is in chains.' Now he had advanced to a state of clarity that only deep calm can provide. This was undoubtedly a wage of fear, as the author's state of mind had shifted from extreme stress caused by external hostility to a radical relaxation. It is irrelevant that Rousseau relapsed into black moods soon afterwards, as demonstrated by his paranoid attacks against his benefactor David Hume. After ceasing to be Rousseau for one happy moment, he had entirely become Rousseau once more, the miserable, the offended, the hunted. Though the altitude of Lake Biel does not match that of Nietzsche's Lake Silvaplana, on whose shores the idea of Zarathustra formed a hundred years later, Rousseau's best intuitions are likewise situated a few thousand feet beyond humans and time. The ultimate goal of what the Americans, in the Declaration of Independence, call the 'pursuit of happiness' had already been temporarily realized on Swiss soil. This shows why the suspicion of the rest of the world towards Switzerland was well-earned: experiences of freedom were conceptualized on the shores of its lakes, and were subversive enough to supply the next thousand years with provocations.

As far as Rousseau is concerned, one can observe that in his way, he had reached the endpoint of every possible revolt against the tyranny of the real. With the fleeting, but at times perfect relief from concern, stress and reality, pure subjectivity subversively comes to light. In the primal scene of the subject, it revealed itself as an exemplary good-for-nothing, unworldly and unusable – more happy animal than *Übermensch*, more dreamer than character, more emigrant than world-improver, more holidaymaker than entrepreneur. The subjectivity released while fleeing from pursuit by the real – the pure feeling of existence removed from all topics – reached, just this once, the pole of complete freedom from stress. Where there is no domineering topic, there is no concern, and where there is no concern, there is no reality.

But if the new freedom goes so far as casting off the weight of the objective as a whole, the reaction from reality will not be long in coming. The concept of reality as such now takes on a reactive undertone, perhaps even a restorative one. The moderns have only known what reality is since the short-lived success of their attempt to cast off its weight. Reality now means objectivity, which returns after the successful retreat to pure subjectivity. That which comes back from temporary oblivion and stakes its claims is perceived as reality. In the networked world, one would advise users that they would be better off using the programme Reality 2.0.

Since it was proved that reality can be forgotten, it has needed advocates to argue for its return. In fact, the European history of ideas and mindsets for the last two hundred and fifty years has essentially been a struggle against the consequences of Rousseau's discovery. It is the endless battle of realism against what has, since then, been termed 'Romanticism', usually in a derisive or warning tone. In this quarrel it is primarily the advocates of reality who hold the floor. In their summings-up, they argue that the moments of detachment among individuals should be considered meaningless, and that the spectre of freedom should be banished from polite company – which from now on means the realists' club.

To express it in a dramatic image: the subject of

the 'Fifth Walk' is like a nuclear reactor that suddenly radiates pure anarchic subjectivity into the environment. In contrast to physical radioactivity, for which we have no sensorium, the radioactivity of the subject is immediately detected by its kind. The reverie of the one provokes the reverie of the other. The manifest freedom of the one involuntarily addresses the other's potential for freedom – especially when the attractiveness of that state is illustrated effectively in literary media. As soon as the complete dissolution of stress takes place in one exemplary individual, its infectious declaration via literature leads many others to ask themselves about the state of dissolution in their own cases. Modernity always strives towards final loosening; that is why reading modern literature cannot be harmless. Where its influence unfolds unhindered, it triggers a chain reaction that could eventually contaminate the whole of society with its radiation unless subjectivity-damping measures are taken in time. As things stand, this can only mean freedom-damping and stress-securing measures. We understand why the drama can only unfold in this order: if the primary subject of the new freedom is the reverie subject, released from social stress, drifting along with no be a small majority who are only mildly affected, which is why their endangered moments barely exceed carefree days off and alcohol-induced dimmings of the real. On the other hand, there are significant groups with high contamination levels among artists, who present themselves as the avant-gardes of uselessness, but also among members of therapeutic professions, providers of relaxation techniques and meditative retreats, as well as exponents of new, comfortable religions – and especially in the youth scenes that established themselves increasingly aggressively in the course of the twentieth century. They have long succeeded in further developing old-fashioned reverie into a veritable culture of disconnected states – words like 'flipping', 'bumming', 'hanging around', 'procrastinating' and 'chilling' act as ciphers for a highly nuanced active inactivity on the fringes of established reality zones. In the twentieth century, all of these areas saw the emergence of countless individuals who acquired alarmingly extensive experience of dissolving reality through relaxation and dissolving society through freedom from stress. It is astonishing in the extreme that there are societies which succeed in integrating the countless strangers that

4

The Reaction of the Real

For some decades, it has been an intellectual fashion to term all sorts of factors in our jointly inhabited world 'constructs' in order to remove their semblance of naturalness and self-evidence. In such contexts, 'society' is always presented as the universal constructor. It is thus taken for granted that one can speak of the social construction of needs, the social construction of childhood, the social construction of sexuality, the social construction of femininity and even the social construction of the menopause. Naturally, this way of thinking does not spare philosophical or metaphysical concepts: it was inevitable that the social construction of nature and the social construction of reality would also be examined.

All these discourses were seemingly in the service of a growing awareness of the achievements of subjectivity. In the modern culture of reflection, people suddenly wanted to see the active subject involved in all matters that had formerly been left to 'nature' or 'objective being'. As is well-known, pre-modern anthropology was infused with the still unshakeable conviction that for all their poetry and striving, humans were ultimately weak, marginal and meaningless – which is why they always needed the safety of a superhuman principle, be it God or the cosmos.

In the following, I will hint at why references to the social construction of reality have an entirely different meaning from that intended by the users of constructivist jargon. Reality is, in fact, a construct in modernity, but precisely not a construct of the subject so much as a construct of the defenders of objectivity that serves no other purpose than to prevent the escape of the subject from the shared stress reality. This is already clearly manifest in the primal scene on Lake Biel: the stone-throwers of Môtiers are already agents of anti-subjective reaction who perceive Rousseau's eccentric appearance in Armenian garb as an act of subversive wilfulness in the midst of all that is solid for them. But, because the radiation of subjectivity, once set in motion, could not be done away with by throwing stones, other means were required to avert the danger emanating from the divine uselessness of the self-immersed reverie subject. These means could only be provided by thinking subject-controllers. These were initially recruited from the German philosophy of the post-Rousseau generation around 1800. Their protagonists had immediately understood intuitively that the new subject was simply not fit for society. With presence of mind, they recognized that their task was to resocialize it in any way they could. This could only be achieved by tailoring a role in the world of achievements to the detached daydreaming subject after all, against its own tendencies. Immanuel Kant – who saw Rousseau as a second Newton – became the first to achieve this by carrying out the turn towards the subject, though only to use the subject for all tasks connected to acts of knowing and judging. From that moment on, its happy unemployment was a thing of the past. Kant had pulled the dreamer off the boat and recruited him for the civil service. It was only now that the subject changed from the servant to the master, from the lying to the noun lacking any substance. Henceforth, no one should escape the labour camp of society. Thus the founder of positivism, August Comte, taught around 1850 that no one had any right except the right to do one's duty. At roughly the same time, the hearty materialist Carl Vogt wrote that thoughts were to the brain as urine to the kidneys. It followed from this that a person who became aware of their existence and articulated it in floating thoughts was in fact merely relieving themselves inwards – an activity to which even a strict employer need not object, provided it is not unduly drawn out. At that point, German liberals were still singing 'Thoughts are free, who can guess them?' No, said the naturalists: thoughts are not free, and one does not need to guess them if one knows the newspaper from which they entered one's head.

This is not the place to lay out the entire history of the disciplining, re-employment, forced socialization and ultimately the slander, denial and annulment of the subject in the cultural development of the nineteenth and twentieth centuries. It would yield the novel of modernity, and modernity fears its most important discovery. Suffice it to say that the inquisition against the relieved subject in recent decades seems to have reached its final stage; for now the neurosciences have appeared on the scene, and their spokespeople, equipped with colourful encephalograms, prove that we are all no more than epiphenomena of neuronal processes, products of an over-interpretation of brain states and parasites on the user interface of neocortices. This view would necessarily make us visitors to a nerve theatre, duped by evolution, unable to help falling for the phantoms on the screen of inwardness.

From the perspective developed here, all reactions to the discovery of subjectivity only seemingly have a philosophical meaning. Rather, I would say that they serve primarily to protect reality, or the sphere of objectivity, against its invalidation in subjective carefreeness. Whether they liked it or not, people had to acknowledge the threat to social cohesion posed by the subject's stress-free ecstasy and ensure the recharging of the social stress field through suitable measures. The only way for this to happen was for the controllers to think of a way of re-conveying subjectivity through objectivity. The aim was to re-implant reality as a stress source in the relaxed subject; this required explaining the nature of the subject's freedom to it in a different way. One had to show it somehow that freedom is the opposite of carefreeness. Freedom, Hegel cunningly states, is the recognition of necessity. Without lifting his head, the man in the boat replies: 'Pull the other one!'

And yet the subject that had drifted away needed to be brought back to the sphere of objective concerns and collective topics. The realists somehow had to pave an acceptable way back for it into the world of stress affairs. The withdrawn subject was therefore given its own access to the sphere of objective efforts by attributing to it a spontaneous inclination towards expansion into the open, work performance, the striving for the object of desire, the conquest of riches, entrepreneurship, the expression of opinions, the battle for recognition and so on – or, one could also say, by giving it a will to stress and wrestling with the external from birth, or at least from the boat. That is the meaning of expressionism, which pervades modern anthropology. By conceiving humans as expressive beings, one ties them internally to the joint construction of the real.

This takes us to the source of the equally suggestive and worthless distinction between negative and positive freedom. In A-level essays and Advent sermons, these are often placed in opposition to each other as 'freedom from' and 'freedom to'. It would have sufficed to consult Rousseau on this matter; he would only have shaken his head at positive freedom. Did he not state that human freedom lies not in the ability to do what one wants, but in not having to do anything one does not want? Did he not owe his most valuable insight to a moment in which he had disembarked from the great galley of reality, including that of 'self-realization'? It is no coincidence that he chose a small boat for the moment of separation, one that drifted on the tide, driven neither by him nor by its own power. There was no room in that boat for internally originating stressors such as will, drive, entrepreneurial spirit, striving for distinction or recognition or such like.

The realization of the negativity of freedom, which follows from translating the theory of freedom into the language of stress theory, has been obscured in contemporary culture since the positive and realistic parties took command. Even in recent times, however, there has not been a complete absence of voices making the case for freedom as a reject of forced burden, especially after the spread of Indian and Far Eastern wisdom traditions in the West. Next to Schopenhauer and the young Sartre, the author who advanced the subject on Western foundations most prominently is Samuel Beckett; one could read his entire output as an essay on the birth of freedom from a general strike against the impositions of the real. This applies especially to Beckett's first, almost forgotten play from 1947, which tellingly bears the title *Eleutheria*. There it is again, the Greek word for freedom, of which we saw earlier that it possessed the purely defensive meaning of a right to remain unmolested by tyrannies, whether of native or Persian origin. Beckett transferred this term carefreely to the modern world by turning the anti-tyrannical precept of Greek *polis* life into an existential principle. In this case one can speak of a productive misunderstanding.

The hero or anti-hero of his play is a young man ironically bearing the triumphant name Victor, a distant relative of Melville's Bartleby, the writer, Goncharov's Oblomov and Xavier de Maistre, who travelled around his room in forty-two days in 1790. We learn from the conversations of the other characters that he withdrew to his room two years ago and has stayed there, cutting off all contact with his family and his fiancée, to say nothing of the rest of the outside world. Victor is a peculiar sort of freedom fighter who strives to break away from reality as such. At the decisive point in the play, he makes an existential confession in which one can easily discern a distant echo of the scene on Lake Biel, transposed into a darker register:

> It won't take a minute. I've always wanted to be free. I don't know why. Nor do I know what it means, to be free. You could tear out all my fingernails and I still couldn't tell you. But far away from words I know what it is. I've always desired it. I still desire it. I desire only that. First I was the prisoner of others. So I left them. Then I was the prisoner of self. That was worse. So I left myself. […] I have nothing more to tell you.'[13]

When the audience member in the piece subsequently asks Victor, 'And death plain and simple, that doesn't speak to you in any way?', Victor

---

[13] Samuel Beckett, *Eleuthéria*, trans. Michael Brodsky (New York: Foxrock, 1996), pp. 162f.

replies: 'If I was dead I wouldn't know I was dead. That's the only thing I've got against death. I want to squeeze pleasure out of my death. That's where freedom lies: seeing oneself dead.'[14] But then he continues: 'I'm giving up on being free. One can't be free. I was mistaken. I can't lead this life any more. [..] One cannot see oneself dead.'[15] The audience member triumphantly interjects:

AUDIENCE MEMBER You can no longer stay like this?

VICTOR No, I no longer can.

AUDIENCE MEMBER It's overtaxing you?

VICTOR Yes.

AUDIENCE MEMBER Well then, be logical. It's either life, with all that it entails of – of subjection, or – the great leave-taking, the real one, to use an image you hold dear. No? […] Or he can return to his family […] come into his inheritance, gratify his fiancée's every whim, start up a magazine, a church, a home of his own, a movie club, and who knows what else? Living or dead, he belongs among us, again he's one of ours.

---

[14] Ibid., p. 166.
[15] Ibid., pp. 167f.

That's all that had to be worked out. That basically there is only us.[16]

Victor later objects to this:

I've changed my mind. [...] I'll never be free. (Pause) But I'll feel myself ceaselessly becoming so. (Pause) My life, I'm going to tell you with what I'll be using it up: with grating my chains against each other. From morning to night and night to morning. That useless little sound, that will be my life. I don't say my joy. Joy, that I leave to you. My calm. My limbo. (Pause) And you come to speak to me of love, of reason, of death! (Pause) Hey, look, go away, go away![17]

Beckett's final stage direction specifies that Victor sits down on his bed and scrutinizes the audience, the orchestra and the balconies on the left and the right. 'Then he gets into bed, his scrawny back turned on mankind.'[18]

[16] Ibid., pp. 168f.
[17] Ibid., pp. 184f.
[18] Ibid., p. 191.

5

On the Source of Committed Freedom

What follows from these memories of the source of modern freedom in the disengagement of the subject from the sphere of shared or objective concerns? One consequence seems an immediate certainty: we cannot do away with the modern experience of freedom described in the 'Fifth Walk' and negativistically expanded upon by Beckett in *Eleutheria*. Neither can we cling fast to the stance of an unconditional holiday and a general strike against objectivity. Most importantly, however, it is impossible for us to repeat Rousseau's own dissolution of the disharmony between subjective reverie and the demands of public life. The unnerving Swiss thinker famously suggested subsuming the freedom of the individual under a homogeneous collective will. In this way, real individual freedom was sacrificed for a fictitious freedom in group subjectivity. For today's observers, there is no doubt that Rousseau's hastily formulated concept of *volonté générale* was the logical nucleus of the socialist fascisms that duelled against their nationalist rivals during the twentieth century. Rousseau had already formulated his fatal idea in his 1762 text about *The Social Contract* before producing the valid form of the new understanding of subjectivity in the 'Fifth Walk' of 1777, written one year before his death. This, admittedly, only proves that even distinguished thinkers do not always gain their most far-reaching insights in the right order. Rousseau should have retracted his doctrine of *volonté générale* in the light of his experience on Lake Biel. His failure to do so was disastrous for the modern world, in which nothing is as irresistible as a wrong idea in heads that seem only to have been waiting for it.

The potential contained in the idea of *volonté générale* came to light a few years after Rousseau's death in the Jacobin terror. The excesses of the Russian and Chinese revolutions revealed how far the madness of the idea of unity would extend.

The deeds of the Khmer Rouge likewise had unde-
niable Rousseauist origins; they reflected what
Pol Pot had learned in Paris between 1949 and
1953. Even in our times, Gaddafi's Libyan social-
ism brought to light aspects of the phantasm that
the will of the whole should be unanimous, and is
best embodied in a chosen individual who wants
to be all things to all people.

What the exposure of subjectivity means for
our understanding of freedom remains a subject
of negotiation in modern civilization to this day.
The last word has not yet been spoken on this
matter, and after what I have discussed here, one
understands why it was impossible to find it.
When the Chinese Prime Minister Zhou Enlai,
in the late Mao era, was asked by a journalist
for his thoughts on the French Revolution, Enlai
hesitated for a moment before stating that it was
still too early to say anything about it. Anyone
required to say something about the individualistic civilization of our time would probably be
equally premature. It is not too early to assess the
state of the freedom problem and its meaning
for the future of human collectives. One need
only look at the current world scene to observe to
what extent the two primary unfreedoms are still

in power. The majority of humans on the planet still have rebellion against political tyranny ahead of them. Virtually all present-day people continue to experience the dictatorship of the real – in fact, they have experienced their oppression more than ever since the real took on the form of globalized traffic and simultaneously evaporated into the phantoms of financial speculation. One can say that the despotism of collective stress constructs is more clearly developed today than at any earlier time, because modernity's revolt against oppression by objectivity resulted in paradoxical subsequent costs that, in some ways, feel more oppressive than the initial burden.

In this situation it is indispensable to reach a new understanding about the meaning of individual freedom and liberal civilization. If pure subjectivity at the freedom end of the spectrum consisted of no more than the individual floating out of all stress fields, it would be identical to strict asociality. That would make liberalism, to quote Martin Walser, an ideology for people who no longer need one another. Then the containment of the asocial through the social would be the last horizon of politics – and the necessary the Greeks called *thymós*. This term referred to an inner affective centre that motivates people to reveal themselves to their social surroundings as owners of giving virtues. Yes: *thymós*, as a liberal mentality of the giving life, offers the only declaration of freedom that has nothing to fear from any naturalistic reduction to exogenous causes and neurological conditions. People have usually searched for freedom in places where one cannot possibly find it – in the will, in the act of choice or in the brain – and overlooked its origin in the noble disposition, in uplift, in generosity. In reality, freedom is simply another word for nobleness, by which I mean the mindset which takes the better and more difficult as its point of reference under any circumstances, precisely because it is free enough for the less possible, the less vulgar, the less all-too-human. In this sense, freedom is availability for the improbable. Freedom still remains true to its essential negativity in the turn towards practical action, because everything it does expresses its rejection of the tyranny of the most probable. Whoever acts out of freedom revolts against the meanness they can no longer bear to see. This freedom is the opposite of everything envisaged by those who see it as a licence to let themselves go into the ordinary, all-too-ordinary.

Should there ever be an intellectual regeneration of political liberalism, it would have to follow from the realization that humans are not simply beings that want to have, creatures driven by greed, addiction and need that demand free rein for their feelings of deficiency and hunger for power. They equally hold the potential for a behaviour that wants to give, and is generous and self-possessed. Pointing this out has never been more important than it is today. Never before have such terms as 'liberal' or even 'neo-liberal' taken on as nefarious a connotation as in the last few years. Never before has liberal thought, especially in our country, been so far from the noble pole of human possibilities. Never before has freedom been so narrowly and fatally associated with the possession of humans by the stress of greed. But what does that prove? One thing alone: that the cause of liberality is too important to be left to the liberals. This restriction does not apply only to a single political party; the cause of the real and its reform is too important to be left to parties. Caring for cultural tradition is thus too comprehensive a task to be entrusted merely to conservatives. The question of preserving the environment is too significant to be considered only a matter for the green parties.. The search for social balance is too demanding for social democrats and leftists to be given sole responsibility for it. Yet each of these elemental motifs requires one main party voice.

As far as defending freedom is concerned, it is a project that cannot dispense either with parties or partisanship. Whoever has experienced something of freedom knows that the concern is still to push back the two tyrannies: the one bearing the face of a despot and the anonymous one that seeks to impose itself as the respectively dominant form of the necessary. We must come to terms with the fact that reality usually surrounds us as an encompassing stress construct. Avowed realists are right to insist on the duty to have a sense of reality. The true liberals supplement it with the sense of possibility: they remind us that we cannot know what kinds of things will yet become possible when people find ways to break away from collectively produced coercive constructions. That is precisely why the current world is boundlessly amazing. Despite illiberal setbacks, it is characterized more than ever before by countless infiltrations from the other state, from disengagement, from the lightness of being – infiltrations that introduce increased levels of freedom into the structures of the existing order. We can defend the cause of freedom by working to make the word 'liberalism', which unfortunately stands for a life on the galley of greed at the moment, a synonym for 'generosity' once more – and to make the word 'liberality' a cipher for sympathy with everything that emancipates people from tyrannies of every kind.

Index

INDEX